Needle Felting

Susanna Wallis

Search Press

First published in Great Britain 2012

Search Press Limited
Wellwood, North Farm Road,
Tunbridge Wells, Kent TN2 3DR

Text copyright © Susanna Wallis 2012

Photographs by Paul Bricknell at
Search Press Studios

Photographs and design copyright
© Search Press Ltd 2012

ISBN: 978-1-84448-905-3

Suppliers
If you have difficulty in obtaining any of the
materials and equipment mentioned in this book,
then please visit the Search Press website for
details of suppliers: www.searchpress.com

Printed in Malaysia

Dedication
To Rachel.

Contents

Introduction

Needle felting is a method of sculpting wool into figures
and forms by piercing it hundreds of times using a felting
needle, then adding colour and details. This book will
enable you to use this method to make a variety of
projects packed full of charm and personality.
The selected techniques allow you to transform the
basic raw material of wool fibres into simple
shapes that are transferable into a wide choice
of characters and designs. The basic needle
felting methods shown can be adapted and

allow for plenty of experimentation and variation. I have incorporated some other simple sewing and beading techniques which extend the range of designs, adding to the overall finished effect of the projects. I hope this book is both a source of information and inspiration for you.

Please note these designs are not toys and children may need supervision if they handle these items. Also, anyone needle felting risks getting pricked fingers, so stay alert and keep your eyes focused while you work.

Materials and techniques

Materials

The basic materials and tools required are simple and inexpensive and include felting needles, a foam pad, cushion or needle felting base, sheep fleece, coloured merino wool fibres, felt fabric, wire, beads, buttons, pipe cleaners, pre-felt merino, linen thread, a needle and thread, embroidery thread, yarn and Wensleydale fibres.

Techniques

Using sheep fleece and dyed and combed wool

All the projects in this book start with a sheep fleece, or raw wool, centre. Some have a wire or pipe cleaner armature which is then covered with the fleece. This is suitable as a stuffing material for the centre of each design as it felts quickly and is bulky and very cost-effective. Once a shape is formed, the finer fibred, dyed and combed wool (such as merino) can be added and will cover up the coarse look of the fleece, resulting in a smoother, colourful finish. All sizes given are an approximate guide – you can adapt all sizing to your own specifications.

Basic ball, egg or body shape

Many of the figures in this book start off as a basic shape. Take a small handful of fleece. Pull out the wool fibres into a long strand, then curl it tightly into a bundle. Place the item on a working surface such as a needle felting base, an old cushion or foam block. Needle the wool repeatedly with your felting needle, making sure the needle goes in and out with a straight up and down movement, and that you keep moving the piece around to work at it from all sides. Add more wool in stages, layering and needling in thin strands to achieve the desired size and shape. With continued needling it should start to form a coarse looking, fairly firmly packed shape. Check your sizing and also if the shape is firm enough. The finished shape is important for the final result so it is worth a little extra effort to refine the shaping at this stage. Keep comparing with the photograph of the finished project and amend as you go.

Sausage shape, arm, leg or toadstool base

Shorter arms, legs and bases can be achieved from a firmly felted wool centre. The method is the same as for the ball shape, but you will need to form a sausage shape, wrapping more fibres around in stages and needling it until it is fairly firm.

Using armatures for arms and legs

For figures with longer arms and legs, use a wire or pipe cleaner armature. This will improve the figure's stance, structure and stability. For an individual limb, use fleece pulled into a long thin strand, hold the wire or pipe cleaner in one hand and wind the wool round it. Place it on the foam pad and needle the piece from all angles, adding more strands until the piece is of the correct shape, depth and firmness, then cover with the required colour fibres before attaching to the body.

To make an armature for an animal, form a simple skeleton with a head, arms and legs from pipe cleaners or similar gauge craft or floristry wire. Cover it with fibres and needle felt the shape, being careful to avoid hitting the wire with your needle. Check that the legs are of the same length.

Wire appendages such as tails

These can be attached to firmly felted figures by threading a 12cm (4¾in) length of wire or pipe cleaner on to a very large darning needle. Sew the wire through the figure where needed, going 1cm (³⁄₈in) below the surface. Pull the needle through to the exit point but leave 2cm (¾in) of wire remaining at the entry point. Remove the darning needle and tightly twist the 2cm (¾in) of wire around the longer piece to secure the tail in place. Cover the wire and any holes or gaps with the final wool fibre colour.

Wrapping a pipe cleaner or wire for thinner areas

For areas such as antennae and tails, the aim is to achieve a much thinner effect, so the finer wool fibres in the final colour are used straight away. Pull the wool fibres into a long, fine strand, hold the wire or pipe cleaner in one hand, and closely and very tightly wind the fibres round it, keeping the look as thin as possible. After the tail or antennae is fixed to the figure, secure the fibres by placing the piece on the foam pad and carefully needling the fibres into each other round the wire or pipe cleaner centre. Continue to add very thin strands, covering all the exposed centre.

Flat, thin shapes

Lay long strands of coloured wool fibres in a close spiral on the foam pad. Needle the piece, removing it from the mat after a few minutes and turning it over to work from the other side. Needle it into a flat circle shape, work in from the sides, and continue to add fibres on the top and bottom to ensure the thickness is enough and that it looks fairly smooth.

Details

Details such as eyes and mouth can be added using very small strands of coloured wool fibres, using them as if drawing or painting. Use very small amounts, poking in the fibres, checking the effect and adding more if needed. Remove any mistakes by carefully pulling out the fibres.

Appendages

For ears, noses, beaks, wings, fins and feet, place a bundle of the coloured fibres the size of a medium coin on the foam pad. For ears and similar appendages, needle the wool into a flat bundle, adding fibres and shaping from the outside edges and all angles to form the shape. Keep a few loose fibres at the point where the piece will be attached. For a nose or beak, start with a bundle the same size, formed into a tiny sausage. Keep firming with the needle as usual and taper the shape to a point at the end. Keep some loose fibres at the other end to attach to the main figure or piece. Always check proportions with your figure as you go.

Blending colours

Merino wool comes in many colours and shades but it can be effective if you blend similar colours, resulting in a more natural look, which is more authentic for animal fur and skin tone. You can also achieve a marbled colour effect as in the Fuzzy Fish on page 12. Blending can by done by selecting fibres and carding (combing) them together using two tools similar to dog brushes. You can also look at using fleeces from different coloured breeds for a natural effect.

7

Feltie Mouse

Materials:

Fleece

Merino in black and pink

Pale pink felt fabric

2 black seed beads

Black and pink thread

Tools:

Felting needle

Foam block

Scissors

Sewing needle

Beading needle

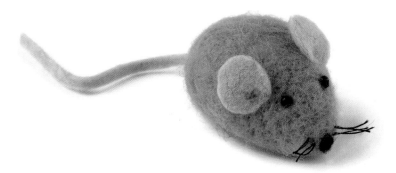

Instructions:

1 Use the needle felting instructions on page 6 to form a low, flat-bottomed egg shape with fleece, tapering it at the end for the nose.

2 Cover the shape with pink merino wool.

3 Cut teardrop-shaped ears and a 9cm (3½in) long strip for a tail from the pink felt fabric.

4 Take the felt ears and check where they will be positioned at the front of the mouse. Take the felting needle and secure each ear in place by needling repeatedly at the point of the teardrop shape. This will make a small indent and will also slightly cup the ear. Take the tail and sew it firmly into place at the back of the mouse body using the sewing needle and pink thread.

5 For the whiskers, thread the sewing needle with black thread. Do not knot the end. Sew into one side of the nose leaving a 2cm (¾in) strand at the entry site. Pull through to the opposite side through the nose, double back through to the original entry site and then back out of the second hole. Cut the thread, leaving a 2cm (¾in) strand. Repeat three times.

6 Needle felt some black wool for the nose.

7 Use a beading needle to sew on black seed beads for the eyes.

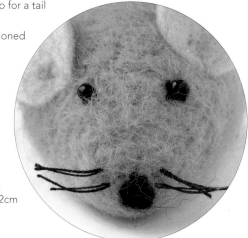

Sugar Mice

Pink and white are traditional colours for sugar mice, but you could also make a grey mouse that is closer to the real thing!

Apple Feltie

Materials:

Fleece

Blended tones of green merino wool plus white, black, green and red

Thick brown felt fabric strip for the stalk

Tools:

Felting needle

Foam block

Scissors

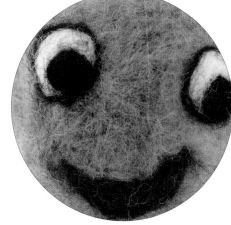

Instructions:

1 Using the needle felting instructions on page 6, bundle some fleece and make a ball shape approx 4cm (1½in) in diameter. Form a flat bottom for the apple to sit on.

2 Needle a dip at the top where the stalk will go.

3 Take some blended merino fibres in different greens and cover the apple.

4 Cut a thin strip of thick brown felt for the stalk and needle it into place.

5 Needle the facial details using white and black merino for the eyes and red and black for the mouth.

Red and Delicious
Make the apple using blended red, green and orange merino fibres.

Fuzzy Fish

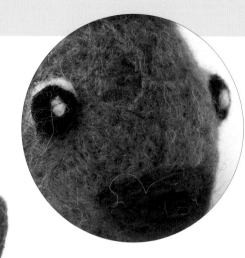

Materials:

Fleece

Blended purple and pink
tones of merino wool
plus black, white, red
and blue

Tools:

Felting needle

Foam pad

Instructions:

1 Use the needle felting instructions on page 6 to form the basic fish body
shape from fleece, making it around 6.5cm (2½in) long. It should be egg-shaped
with a slightly flat bottom. Keep adding fibres until the shape, density and size
are as required.

2 Shape the dorsal (back) fin and the tail pieces separately in fleece and
cover them with the blended merino fibres. Leave the fibres looser where the
pieces will be attached to the fish. Attach them firmly using the felting needle
and working from all angles. Add extra coloured fibres where necessary to
strengthen the join and disguise any gaps.

3 Cover the whole fish with blended marble effect fibres in pink and purple
tones of merino wool.

4 Gauge where the eyes will go. Using black merino wool, make two eyes and
add some white. Add a red mouth and blue lips.

Something Fishy

Blend gold and yellow tones of merino wool fibres to make the alternative fish. This one has red lips instead of blue. Perhaps the water is warmer!

Starfish Feltie

Materials:
Fleece
Yellow merino
Seed beads
Yellow thread

Tools:
Felting needle
Foam block
Beading needle

Instructions:

1 Use the needle felting instructions on page 6 to make five fairly firm sausage shapes approximately 4cm (1½in) long using fleece. Keep one end of each shape more loosely needled.

2 Place the five pieces on to the foam block in a starfish shape with the looser fibre ends overlapping in the middle.

3 Needle felt the five pieces together into a starfish form. Try to achieve a flat base and smooth edges.

4 Once a good shape is achieved, fully cover the starfish in yellow merino by adding small strands and needling until the coverage is even.

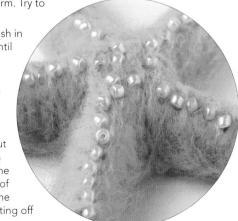

5 Use a beading needle and yellow thread to add a row of beads along each leg of the starfish. Thread the beading needle with doubled yellow thread and tie a knot. Stitch through the leg from the bottom, thread a small bead on to the needle as it emerges on top, pull the needle through, and stitch close to the exit hole but just going under the surface of the leg by around 5mm (¼in). Bring the needle back out again just alongside the first bead, add the next bead and continue until a line of beads is sewn along each leg. Stitch back through to the base once all beading is completed and tie a knot, cutting off all excess thread.

A Couple of Stars

Make another starfish in aqua merino, reminiscent of warm, tropical seas, and decorate it with clear seed beads with an iridescent glow.

Rocking Robin

Materials:

Fleece

Merino in brown and
orange-red

Felt fabric in dark
brown and mid-
brown

2 black seed beads

Brown thread

Tools:

Felting needle

Foam block

Sewing needle

Beading needle

*The templates for the
wings and beak.*

Instructions:

1 Use the needle felting instructions on page 6 to form a
single shape for the bird body and head from fleece, using the
photograph for guidance. Ensure that the body can 'sit' without
wobbling by working on making the base flat.

2 Cover the body and head evenly with brown merino, leaving the face and breast
area free. Then add orange-red fibres to these areas. Needle the fibres so they
smoothly cover the base wool.

3 Use the templates above to cut out two wing shapes from mid-brown felt fabric
and a small diamond for the beak from dark brown felt fabric. Sew the wings on to the
bird using the sewing needle and a couple of stitches in brown thread. Sew across the
middle of the diamond to divide it into the top and bottom of the beak.

4 Use the beading needle and brown thread to sew on black seed beads for the eyes.

Watch the Birdies

*Make an chick in yellow merino, or a
bluebird in pale blue. These needle
felted birds make lovely decorations for
Christmas or Easter.*

Woolly Ewe

Materials:
Fleece
Black merino
Cream woolly yarn
2 black faceted beads
Black thread

Tools:
Felting needle
Foam pad
Beading needle
Sewing needle

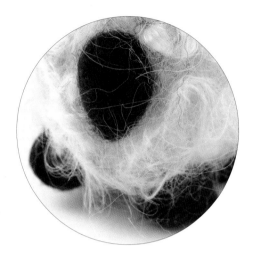

Instructions:

1 Using the needle felting instructions on page 6, form a sturdy body from a basic egg shape using the fleece, approximately 6.5cm (2½in) long.

2 Cut off a long length of the cream woolly yarn and wind it randomly around the body shape, totally covering the body to resemble a curly fleece. Set aside.

3 Take a table tennis ball-sized bundle of black wool. Form it into an oval shape approx 1cm (³/₈in) thick, leaving some fibres longer at one end of the oval, where the ears will be.

4 Form small ears by needling where the longer fibres are. Work in between them so that a dip forms and the ears emerge. Continue shaping around the sides of the ears until defined ear shapes are formed. Use the sewing needle and black thread to sew this head firmly on to the front of the woolly body, keeping the stitching as invisible as possible.

5 Form four 2cm (¾in) long block-shaped feet using black merino. Check they are all of a similar size and sew them underneath the sheep.

6 Attach some black merino at the end of the sheep, shaping it to become a tail.

7 Use a beading needle and black thread to sew two black beads on to the face for the eyes.

I Love Ewe Mum

Make a sweet sleeping lamb to sit alongside the ewe, using Jacob or similar grey wool. You don't need to add legs as the lamb is lying down.

Fuzzy Bunny

Materials:
Fleece
Grey and white merino
2 black seed beads
Black thread

Tools:
Felting needle
Foam block
Beading needle
Sewing needle

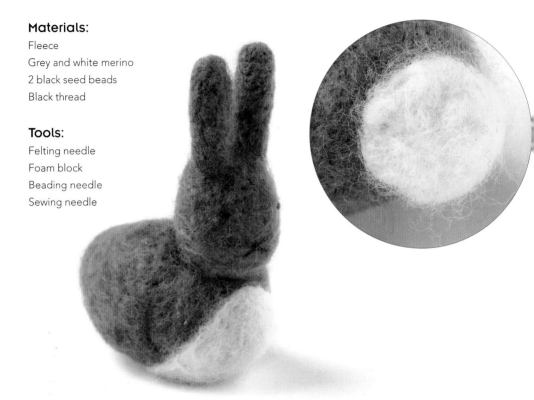

Instructions:

1 Using the instructions on page 6, form a 4cm (1½in) egg-shaped body from fleece and give it a flattened base.

2 Make a ball for the head and needle it into place. Needle the figure until fairly firm and cover it with grey merino.

3 Make two firm sausage-shaped ears 3cm (1¼in) long, using the grey merino. Keep some loose fibres at one end. Position the ears on the head, making sure you are happy with their placement. Needle the ears into the head using the loose fibres. Add more fibres as needed to secure the ears firmly and hide any gaps at the joining point.

4 Add the tummy by needle felting with white merino. For the tail take a large coin-sized bundle of white merino and form into a small ball approximately 1cm (³⁄₈in) wide. Place it in position and needle it in place, adding more fibres if it becomes too flat.

5 Use the beading needle and black thread to sew on seed beads for eyes. Use the sewing needle to make a cross stitch in black thread for the mouth.

Hop It!
These two felted friends would make perfect Easter bunnies for a seasonal display.

Feltie Feline

Materials:

Fleece

Merino in fudge brown, pink and green

Pipe cleaner

2 black seed beads

Black thread

Tools:

Felting needle

Darning needle

Foam pad

Beading needle

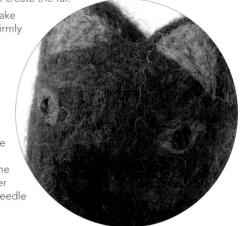

Instructions:

1 Use the needle felting instructions on page 6 to form a long egg shape from fleece around 7cm (2¾in) high. Flatten it on one end so it has a stable surface to stand on. One quarter down from the top, taper the shape to make a neck, creating a fairly wide head at the top.

2 Cover the whole figure in the fudge brown merino to create the fur.

3 Follow the *Appendages* instructions on page 7 to make two triangular ears using the same colour merino and firmly attach them to the top of the head.

4 Add eye shapes using green merino and inner ears using pink. Use a beading needle and black thread to sew on two seed beads for pupils.

5 Attach a pipe cleaner at the tail end using the *Wire appendages such as tails* technique shown on page 7. Once secured, cover the pipe cleaner in the same fur colour. Pull the fudge brown wool fibres into a long, fine strand and wind them tightly round the pipe cleaner, keeping the look as thin as possible. Place the cat on the foam pad and carefully needle the fibres into each other round the pipe cleaner. Cover any wire that shows by needle felting in over it. Curl the tail into shape.

Puss, Puss!

Felt is ideal for creating our furry friends. The alternative cat has been made lying down, with orange eyes.

Perky Penguin

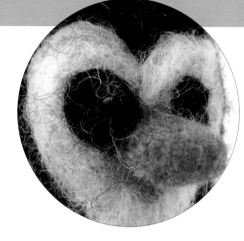

Materials:

Fleece

Merino in white, black and orange

Orange felt fabric

Strong thread

2 black seed beads

Black and orange thread

Tools:

Felting needle

Foam pad

Sewing needle

Beading needle

The templates for the wings (top) and feet (bottom).

Instructions:

1 Using the needle felting instructions on page 6, needle the fleece into an egg shape with a flattened base. Make a small ball shape for the head, checking proportions with the base. Attach the ball to the top of the egg shape by needling from all angles to ensure it is firmly secured and adding extra fleece fibres to cover any gaps. The total height should be around 6.5cm (2½in).

2 Cover the front of the figure with the white merino wool. Then using the black, cover the rest of the bird, leaving white for the belly area and a white heart shape for the face.

3 Make a beak from orange merino using the *Appendages* technique shown on page 7 and fix this to the face.

4 Use the template above to cut out feet from orange felt fabric and sew these on with orange thread underneath the base.

5 Use the wing template as a guide to help you form wings separately on the foam pad, using white merino underneath and black on top. Follow the instructions for *Appendages* on page 7. Leave some fibres loose at the end and needle these on to the body of the bird.

6 Add eyes with black fibres and finish off by sewing on black seed bead pupils using a needle and black thread.

It's Freezing!
*Use a grey sheep fleece
such as Jacob to make this
cute penguin chick.*

Tortoise Feltie

Materials:

Fleece

Merino in green, orange,
  black, white and red

Thin yarn

Orange thread

Tools:

Felting needle

Foam block

Sewing needle

Instructions:

1 Use the needle felting instructions on page 6 to form the fleece into a half egg shape with a flat base for the shell of the tortoise.

2 Cover the shell with green merino.

3 Needle felt four sausage shapes from fleece for the legs, following the instructions on page 6. They should be 2cm (¾in) long. Make the feet ends of the legs a little more rounded. Make the head in the same way, but wider and 4cm (1½in) long, with a rounded end for the face. Cover the legs and head with orange merino.

4 Place the shell upside down, put the legs and head into the right position and firmly stitch them in place under the shell using a needle and orange thread and keeping all the stitches invisible where possible.

5 Keeping the tortoise upside down, fill the space between the legs and neck with green merino. Make this shell underside look as smooth as possible by shaping it around the limbs and neck, concealing the stitched joins.

6 Turn the tortoise over and check his standing position.

7 Add facial details: needle felting white eyes with black pupils and a red mouth.

8 To make the texture on the shell, needle felt thin orange yarn in inter-connecting oval shapes. Then shape this even further by working along each yarn line with the felting needle to create an indent, so that the shell is bumpy.

Slow But Sure

Take your time making these tortoise felties, you'll get there in the end! The alternative tortoise is made with blue merino and has a flatter shell, with a slightly different pattern.

Snowflake Doll

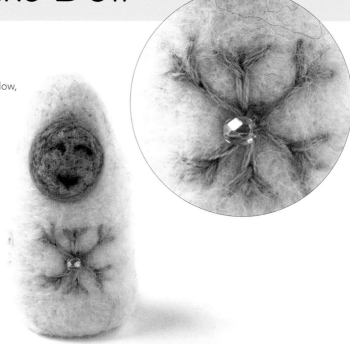

Materials:

Fleece

Merino in white, skin tone, yellow, red, black and pale blue

Pale blue embroidery thread

Pale blue cotton thread

1 faceted pale blue bead

Tools:

Felting needle

Foam block

Sewing needle

Beading needle

Embroidery needle

Instructions:

1 Use the needle felting instructions on page 6 to make a firm sausage shape using fleece with a pointed top and a flattened base, around 7.5cm (3in) high and 3.5cm (1⅜in) in diameter.

2 Cover the doll shape with white merino.

3 Needle on a circle of skin tone merino for the face, and outline this with a ring of pale blue merino. Add yellow merino for the hair and curves for the eyes and mouth in black and red.

4 Thread an embroidery needle with pale blue embroidery thread and tie a knot at the end. Entering from the base of the doll, sew upwards and outwards towards the front of the figure so that the needle emerges 2.5cm (1in) up the body in the centre. Pull the thread through, and judging where you want the stitch to go, position the needle and sew back into the body of the doll. Go about 5mm (¼in) under the surface and come out to begin the next stitch. Continue to sew in and out of the doll to form the snowflake pattern, going 5mm (¼in) under the surface with each stitch. Further snowflakes can be embroidered around the body. Finish by sewing back down to the base, pull the thread through and tie a knot under the base, cutting off any excess thread.

5 Thread a beading needle with blue thread, knot the end and go up through the base of the doll again to come out in the centre front at the centre of the snowflake design. Thread on the bead and take the needle down to the base again and tie off.

Steps for the snowflake embroidery

1

2

3

Primrose and Snowflake

These doll felties represent two of the seasons;
you could design your own summer and autumn
dolls. The spring doll is in primrose yellow with an
embroidered leaf design and yellow beads.

Ladybird Feltie

Materials:
Fleece
Merino in red, black and white
Black linen thread
Black cotton thread
2 black seed beads

Tools:
Felting needle
Foam block
Sewing needle
Beading needle

Instructions:

1 Use the needle felting instructions on page 6 to form a half egg shape with fleece. It should have a high curved bump with a flat base.

2 For the head, make a table tennis ball-sized bundle of black wool, and needle felt it to form a small ball but with a flat base like the body. Compare it to the body to get the right size. Place the head against the body and start to needle through the head into the body to secure it, working from all sides and underneath to ensure a firm join with no gaps.

3 Cover the body with red merino, then needle on three spots on each side with black merino, and a dividing line down the middle, also with black.

4 Add the eye shapes with white merino and sew a black seed bead in the centre of each eye using black cotton thread and a beading needle.

5 Linen or similar firm thread is best for antennae. Thread the linen thread on to a sewing needle and do not make a knot. Position the needle above the eye of the bug, sew into the head, across to the area below the opposite eye. Pull the needle back out but leave a 2.5cm (1in) tail of thread where the needle entered, above the eye. Sew back under the surface towards the first hole and pull out the needle, tugging gently to make the thread taut. Avoid leaving any thread showing and sew back adjacent to the first hole and out to above the second eye. Pull the thread through, leaving a 2.5cm (1in) tail of thread for the second antenna and trim off the excess.

Fuzzy Ted

Materials:

Fleece

Merino in pale blue, white, black and skin tone

Pale blue thread

Tools:

Felting needle

Foam block

Sewing needle

Instructions:

1 Using the needle felting instructions on page 6, form a long body shape with fleece 6cm (2⅜in) high. You then need to form a head shape coming to a quarter of the way down from the top. Start by needling a neckline and shape the head into a wide oval, adding more fleece fibres if needed.

2 For the muzzle area at the front of the face, take a large coin-sized bundle of fleece and shape it with the needle on the foam block into a small egg shape, checking the size in relation to the bear's head. Attach it to the head by needle felting, working from all angles and using extra fibres to hide any gaps or holes at the join, all the while comparing against the photographs to get the shape right.

3 Flatten the body shape at the bottom so that the figure can sit without wobbling. Set it aside. Form four sausage shapes for limbs 4cm (1½in) long, following the instructions on page 6.

4 Wrap some more fibres at the end of each limb and shape them into paws. Cover the body, head and limbs with pale blue merino.

5 Stitch two limbs very firmly in place at the shoulders and two at the hips, using a sewing needle and pale blue thread and keeping all the joining stitches as hidden as possible.

6 Add some ears using the method shown for *Appendages* on page 7.

7 Needle felt inner ears, the muzzle and paw prints with skin tone merino, then add white eyes with black centres and a nose and mouth in black.

Russian Dolls

Materials:

Fleece

Merino in skin tone and an
assortment of bright colours

Tools:

Felting needle

Foam pad

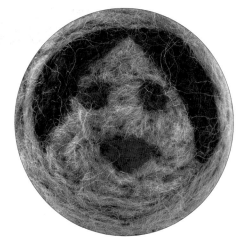

Sizes:

If you are making the whole family of
dolls, make the smallest first, then form
each doll to be slightly bigger than the
last one. My smallest doll is 3cm (1¼in)
high, and the tallest is 7cm (2¾in) high.

Instructions:

1 Using the needle felting instructions on page 6, needle a fleece bundle
into an egg shape with a flattened end for standing. Check that the doll
is firmly felted enough and stands up straight and set it aside.

2 Continue with the other dolls, gradually increasing them in size. Cover
each doll with its bright merino base colour.

3 Needle a circle for the face on each doll, with skin tone merino. Add a
colour frame around the face, then brown hair, blue eyes and red mouths.

4 Finally add the dots in merino to contrast with the base colours.

Family of Five

These dolls are made from a simple shape, so are easy to form. The fun is all in the decoration. Choose colours that really zing together like the lime green and hot pink of the largest doll.

Toadstool Feltie

Materials:

Fleece

Merino wool in white and red

White thread

Tools:

Felting needle

Foam pad

Sewing needle

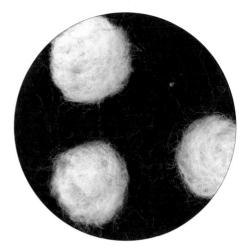

Instructions:

1 Use the needle felting instructions on page 6 to make a cone shape with fleece 5cm (2in) high for the toadstool's stalk. Start with a sausage shape, add fibres to one end and taper it at the other end. Make sure the base is wide enough so that the toadstool does not topple over.

2 Cover the stalk with white merino. Set the piece aside.

3 Spiral thick red merino fibres on the foam pad to make a circle 5cm (2in) in diameter. Follow the instructions for *Flat, thin shapes* on page 7. Continue needling the fibres to form a firm-edged red circle.

4 Add white fibres to make the underside of the toadstool and continue needling to create a firm circle.

5 Once the circle is firm, stitch the toadstool base firmly to the top using a sewing needle and white thread. Cover any visible stitches by needle felting over them in white.

6 Add white spots on the red top of the toadstool.

Felted Fungi
Create the other fungus with mushroom-coloured merino and a golden-brown top. You could make your own forest floor in felt!

Perky Pig

Materials:

Fleece
Merino in pink, brown and black
Pipe cleaners
2 black seed beads
Black thread

Tools:

Felting needle
Foam pad
Scissors
Beading needle

Instructions:

1 Using the instructions on page 7, make a simple animal armature using pipe cleaners, checking that the legs are the same length.

2 Wrap fleece around the wire body, legs and head parts and begin to needle the wool, adding more wool to achieve a plump shape. Continue to felt, checking against the photographs for guidance and aiming for a nice plump pig shape with a fat tummy and narrow trotters.

3 Check that the head shape is quite long. Add more fibres to make the pronounced snout area. Once you are satisfied with the face shape, work from the front of the face, flattening the snout area, working around so that it is circular in shape. Then form the mouth under the snout by working the needle inwards in a line from the front and from either side.

4 Wrap thin strands of pink merino around the body until fully and evenly covered.

5 Use the template above and the *Appendages* instructions on page 7 to make two ears.

6 For the tail, roll up a very small amount of pink merino and needle it into a very thin string. Needle this on to the tail area and create a twist as you attach the tail.

7 Using a small amount of brown merino, create a line through each of the pig's feet to divide them into trotters. Use black merino to make nostrils. Sew on two black seed beeds for eyes using a beading needle and black thread.

Pig's ear template.

Caterpillar Feltie

Materials:

Fleece

Merino in green, yellow,
   purple, red, blue, orange,
   black and white

Pipe cleaner

Thick thread

Tools:

Felting needle

Foam pad

Large darning needle

Instructions:

1 Following the instructions on page 6, take a bundle of fleece and needle felt it into a ball shape until it is fairly firm and 3cm (1¼in) in diameter. This will be the head of the bug.

2 Cover the head with thin strands of green merino wool and needle felt until it is smooth. Set it aside.

3 Repeat with yellow, purple, red and blue balls, making each one slightly smaller than the previous one. For the tail, make a small carrot shape, one end flat and the other pointed, and cover with orange merino.

4 Thread a pipe cleaner on to a large darning needle to insert the antennae in the head. Push the darning needle through the ball and out the other side to where the other antenna will be, leaving a length of 4cm (1½in) for each antenna. Wind thin strands of black merino round the antennae and needle them into place following the *Wrapping a pipe cleaner or wire for thinner areas* instructions on page 7.

5 Curl the antennae into shape. Needle the wool around the entry point of each one carefully to hold the antennae in place.

6 Place the head and other balls in order with the orange carrot shape at the end. Thread a large darning needle with embroidery thread and stitch into the back of the head. Pull the thread back out 1cm (³⁄₈in) away, still at the back of the head. Sew through the centre of all the other ball shapes and the tail, pulling firmly between each one to bring them close together. If it is difficult to pull the needle through, you can use jewellery pliers.

7 Tie a knot at the end of the tail, cut off excess threads and disguise the knot by needle felting over it with orange merino fibres.

8 For the face of the bug add two small bundles of green merino to form eyeballs and add the white and black eye details, plus a red mouth.

Ugly Bug Ball

This alternative needle feltie bug has just one body section and is covered in bright spots.

41

Fuzzy Owl

Materials:

Fleece

Merino in claret, black, cream, toffee, grey, black and white

Tools:

Felting needle

Foam block

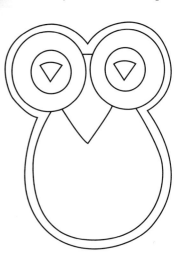

The template for the owl design.

Instructions:

1 Use the needle felting instructions on page 6 to make an oval body shape from fleece with a flat base and some extra fibres at the top. It should be 7cm (2¾in) high.

2 Create the owl shape using the extra fibres at the head end and concentrating on needling a dip in the middle of the head. Form the pointed ears in this way and shape them until firm.

3 Cover the owl in claret merino.

4 Using the template as a guide, create black eyes with large cream circular outlines and white triangles in the centre. Make a diamond-shaped beak in toffee merino between the eyes, and a grey oval-shaped tummy below. Outline all these deatils in black merino.

What a Hoot!

The owl chick is made with beige merino with a brown tummy and bright yellow beak.

Feltie Elf

Materials:

Fleece

Merino in green, red, white, skin tone and dark brown

White felt fabric

Dyed Wensleydale curly wool fibre

White embroidery thread

Tools:

Felting needle

Scissors

Sewing needle

Instructions:

1 Use the needle felting instructions on page 6 to make a sausage shape from fleece, with a flattened bottom, approximately 7cm (2¾in) high. To make a head, taper in around a quarter of a way down the figure, needle a ball shape at the top and continue needling to define this head shape and the neck.

2 Cover the body with green merino.

3 Cover the head with skin tone merino. Decide where the face will go and needle some curly Wensleydale fibres on the rest of the head for hair.

4 Needle felt a toadstool design using red and white merino on the front of the body. Add a red hat with white spots and a green border. Needle felt two dark brown eyes and a red mouth on the face.

5 Cut a zigzag collar from white felt fabric, long enough to go round the neck of the figure. Thread a needle with white embroidery thread but do not tie a knot. Stitch along the straight line of the collar, leaving a length of thread at the entrance and at the other end. Pull the threads at either end to gather the collar up and tie the collar round the neck of the figure, securing it with two knots. Cut of any excess thread.

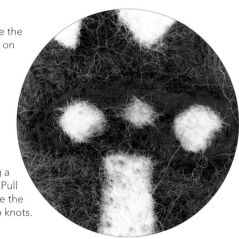

Nordic Beauty

This alternative feltie doll has a
Scandinavian feel, with Wensleydale wool
in a blond shade and subtle pastel colours.

Feltie the Snowman

Materials:

Fleece

Merino in white, orange and dark brown

White and red thread

Red felt fabric

Wire birds' legs (from craft supplier) painted black or made with craft wire

2 faceted beads

Strong clear glue

Tools:

Felting needle

Foam block

Large darning needle

Sewing needle

Scissors

Beading needle

Instructions:

1 Make three fleece balls in descending size. The largest ball will need a flattened base.

2 Using a large darning needle and white thread, sew the balls together and cover any joins by needling white merino over the gaps to give a smooth finish.

3 Take a handful of brown merino fibres and needle them into three small circles going down the snowman's body for buttons, adding fibres as needed. For the mouth, needle a very thin strand of dark brown merino into place.

4 For the carrot nose, follow the instructions for *Appendages* on page 7 with orange merino. Keep some fibres loose at the joining end and attach it to the snowman's face. Try to taper the point of the carrot as much as possible. If you needle felt the nose hard enough and the wool is very compact, you may even be able to trim it very carefully to a sharp point with scissors.

5 Sew on beads for the eyes using the beading needle and white thead.

6 Cut a scarf from red felt fabric, with tiny cuts at the end for a fringed effect, tie in a knot and sew into place using red thread.

7 Using a very narrow point from a pair of scissors or the darning needle, poke a hole where an arm will go on the snowman's body.

8 Add a dab of strong clear glue at the hole site and push in the wire arm so that the wire is half inside and quite firm. Add a dab more glue. Repeat for the other arm and allow to dry.

Chilly Chap

The shorter snowman is made from one ball for the body and one for the head, and he has a real button decoration.

Acknowledgements

Thanks to Roz and Sophie at Search Press; this was a fun project to work on. Thanks also to my family for enduring the wool mountain that sometimes threatens to take over my home. Thanks to those friends new and old in the UK, Germany, the USA and Singapore, whose support and belief in me have given me the strength to rise above challenges.

Publisher's Note

If you would like more information about needle felting, try *Beginner's Guide to Needle Felting* by the same author, Search Press, 2008